AL-MUNĀJAH
The Intimate Discourse

AL-MUNĀJAH
THE INTIMATE DISCOURSE

Imām Ḥasan al-Banna

Foreword by
Ustādh Ṣayful-Islām al-Banna

Translation & commentary by
Shaykh Aḥmad Muḥammad Sa'ad

ANGELWING

Title	AL-MUNĀJAH: The Intimate Discourse
ISBN	978-0-9555779-1-8

British Library Cataloguing in Publication Data
A catalogue record of this book is available from The British Library

Editors	Syed Tohel Ahmed & Susanne Thackray
Cover Design	Syed Nuh
Typesetting	Red Aspect

Printed in Turkey

Angelwing Media
www.angelwingmedia.net

Dedication

This book is dedicated to the men and women of our glorious past and to all those who follow in their footsteps by sacrificing time, wealth and their lives in pursuit of Allah's pleasure.

Acknowledgements

Angelwing Media would like to thank all those who provided valuable assistance and guidance during the publication of this book. Ṣayful-Islām al-Banna, son of the late Imām Ḥasan al-Banna for finding the time from his busy schedule to write the foreword; Hanif Osmani, Usamah Ward and Dr. Yeasmin Mortuza for their suggestions; the brothers and sisters of Islamic Forum Europe whose high spiritual aspiration and community activism constantly inspire us; and of course our eternal gratitude to Shaykh Aḥmad Muḥammad Sa'ad for the translation and commentary.

Contents

FOREWORD **13**
TRANSLATORS PREFACE **15**
ABOUT *Al-Munājah* **17**
KEY TO TRANSLITERATION **19**
INTRODUCTION **21**

CHAPTER ONE
The merits and timing of *Qiyāmul-Layl* **23**
Qur'ānic verses *23*
Prophetic aḥādīth *25*
Traditions of the righteous predecessors *27*

CHAPTER TWO
The merits of *du`ā'* and *istighfār* **31**
Qur'ānic verses *31*
Prophetic aḥādīth *32*

CHAPTER THREE
Etiquette and the optimal time for making *du`ā'* **35**
ETIQUETTE
1) Raising one's palms *35*
2) A presence of heart and conviction that Allāh will accept one's du`ā' *36*
3) Praising Allāh *36*
4) Concluding the du`ā' with 'Amīn' *37*
5) A supplicant should be calm and never raise his voice while making du`ā' *37*
6) Choosing short, meaningful and comprehensive expressions (Jawami`al-Kalīm) *37*
7) Repeating one's du`ā' and istighfār three times *37*
8) A person should be patient in receiving an answer (for his du`ā') *38*
9) Du`ā' should always be made for the benefit of the supplicant, his children and his belongings *38*
10) Upon making du`ā' for someone else, a person should start by making du`ā' for himself *38*
THE OPTIMAL TIME FOR MAKING DU`Ā'
1) Between the adhān and iqāmah *38*
2) While performing prostration (sujūd) *39*
3) While on a journey and if one is oppressed *39*
4) When hearing the adhān, during war and when it rains *39*

Chapter Four
Selected *du`ā'* from the Glorious Qur'ān **41**

Chapter Five
On celebrating praise of Allāh and invoking divine blessings upon the Prophet ﷺ **43**
Celebrating praise of Allāh *43*
Invoking divine blessings upon the Prophet ﷺ *43*

Chapter Six
The Prophet's ﷺ *du`ā'* in *Tahajjud* Prayer **46**

Chapter Seven
The Munājah of the Righteous **49**
The Munājah of `Alī ibn Abū Ṭālib *49*
The Munājah of Ibn `Ata'illāh of Alexandria *51*
The Munājah of Aḥmad al-Rifa`ī *53*
The Munājah of Aḥmad ibn Idrīs *54*
The Munājah of Shaykh Abul-Ḥasan al-Shadhilī *55*
The Munājah of Imām al-Shāfi`ī *56*

Chapter Eight
Selected Supplications **57**

Conclusion **59**
Glossary **61**

بسم الله الرحمن الرحيم

Foreword

My late father Imām Ḥasan al-Banna (may Allāh bless his soul) wrote that the crisis of his time was caused by the spiritual and moral decline in society. The truth of this statement is increasingly apparent today. In the modern world, material and scientific advancements have flourished at the expense of spiritual needs. The tyranny, injustices and wars that we see in the world today are a direct result of this void that exists in our lives. Moreover, it is our leaders and rulers who are most in need of spiritual enrichment. They need to comprehend real greatness, which is the securing of peace, safety, and justice for all humanity.

The great challenge of our time is how we overcome the torrent of materialism that has permeated every aspect of our lives hence causing disequilibrium around the globe. Only by elevating man's spiritual inclination – which, in its essence, flows from belief in the One True God, the message of all the prophets and the teachings of the divinely revealed books culminating with the arrival of Prophet Muḥammad ﷺ – can the balance be restored.

This book is the first step on the path to returning to Allāh, the Creator and the Sustainer of all. It explains how through *munājah* (prayer and intimate discourse) one can reconnect to the Creator. Regardless of race, colour, language or location, if one applies the message contained in this book, it will result in the attainment of spiritual enrichment and contentment in one's own life as well as in the lives of fellow human beings.

I call upon Muslims wherever they are to strike a balance between their spiritual and material lives, for only with such balance can contentment be achieved.

Let me seize this opportunity to greet the publishers who commissioned the translation of this treatise for I believe that Allāh has guided them to the right path. It is my belief that the decision to make this treatise available to the English-speaking world sincerely reflects their feelings for Islām. I hope that one day these feelings will be transmitted from their hearts to the hearts of all people so that strength is given to the voice of the soul, the voice of truth and above all, the message of Allāh.

I would also like to thank Aḥmad Sa`ad for his translation and commentary. I believe that it was not an easy job, so I pray that Allāh rewards him abundantly and magnifies his scale of righteous deeds.

Finally, yet importantly, the mission of Imām Ḥasan al-Banna was to put the Muslim *ummah* back on the path to Allāh. He believed that spiritual enlightenment would eventually play its rightful part in shaping our lives. To him, spirituality is the only rope of salvation for society. This book is a humble contribution to help humanity once again draw closer to its Master and Creator.

Ṣaiful-Islām al-Banna
Cairo, 10 May 2008

Translator's Preface

The deeper a man's faith, the more penetrating is his supplication. Words of goodness emanating from a pure and obedient heart reach the peaks of the heavens by the Grace of Allāh and gain His Pleasure and Acceptance.

Allāh is always with His servants as long as they have firm belief and trust in Him. In the divine saying, Allāh informs us: "I am always as My servant thinks of Me and I am with him whenever he remembers Me. If he remembers Me in his heart, I will remember him to Myself. If he mentions My Name in a gathering, I will mention his name in a gathering better than his."

The oppressed, lacking the material arms to defend themselves, still have the weapon of supplication at their side. If worldly means fail to assist, Allāh is the One Who can give them power and victory over their oppressor.

Whenever faced by a problem or difficulty, the Prophet ﷺ would rush to prayer. When the Prophet ﷺ visited Ṭāif, he was subjected to humiliation and torture. He immediately turned to Allāh to supplicate. Emanating from a heart heavy with sadness and distress, his words were: "O Allāh! To You I complain of my weakness, lack of resources and of the humiliation I was subjected to before the people. O Most Merciful of those who show mercy, You are the Lord of the ill treated and You are my Lord. To whom do You entrust me? To some distant stranger who scowls at me? Or to an enemy who has authority over my affairs? As long as You are not angry with me I do not care, but Your grace is more befitting to me. I seek refuge in the light of Your Face by which all darkness is dispelled and rectifies the affairs of this world and the Hereafter against incurring Your wrath or being the subject of your anger. To You is our obedience until You are pleased and there is no might or power except with You."

Our Lord is All-Merciful, Most Kind, the Pardoner and the

Loving. He is closer to you than your own heart. He is more merciful with you than your own mother who gave birth to you. It is your duty then to turn to Him, draw closer to His gates and voice all your concerns in His presence. He will never fail you.

About Al-Munājah

Of all the works of the late Imām Ḥasan al-Banna; the treatise *Al-Munājah* did not receive much acclaim. Many people know it by name but only a few have had the chance to read it. Small in size and clear in language, *Al-Munājah* stands on its own as a piece of writing that touches its readers' hearts and summons their tears. The Arabic text of *Al-Munājah* roughly falls into 63 small pages and was published by Dārul-Shihāb, Egypt.

What is unique about *Al-Munājah* is that it carries a general message; it is for all Muslims rather than just the members of the Muslim Brotherhood. It is a treatise on spiritual themes rather than activism and organisational matters; it is a declaration of the vision and mission of all humanity expressed in a very touching and highly spiritual language.

My work on *Al-Munājah* involved translating the original Arabic text into English, commenting on it, explaining many of its obscurities and verifying the authenticity of the *aḥādīth* mentioned therein. I realised that a difficult task lay before me. Hence, I sought Allāh's help, embarked on the work and was able, by His Grace, to finish it to the best of my knowledge. The addition of a glossary adds to the reader's understanding of specific words, which in the Arabic language can allude to many meanings. Having said this however, I feel that one needs to learn the original language of *Al-Munājah* in order to be able to sense and enjoy the sweetness of its text. Possessing an exquisite eloquence, Arabic stands on its own as a language that can contain meanings and convey messages that cannot otherwise be delivered by any other language. In Arabic, a word carries many nuances beyond being a means of just delivering a certain message.

The author of *Al-Munājah*, Imām Ḥasan al-Banna, was born into a religious family in the Egyptian town of Al-Maḥmudiyyah in 1906. Al-Banna's father received his education at Al-Azhar and was a watch repairer by profession. He instilled strong religious values into the young Ḥasan al-Banna. In 1923, Ḥasan al-Banna moved to Cairo to join the famous Dārul-'Ulūm College. After graduation in 1927, he worked as a primary school teacher in Isma`iliyyah, a city in eastern Egypt. His activism and voluntary work for the revival of religious values and ethical standards endeared him to the hearts of people. It was in this city that al-Banna, along with six other associates – who used to listen to his many lectures – established the Muslim Brotherhood. Since its establishment in 1928, the Muslim Brotherhood has proved to be one of the largest Islāmic organisations in the world. Its leadership in Islāmic *da`wah* work, educating young Muslims and re-introducing Islāmic concepts and values into the minds of the masses are beyond dispute.

In February 1949, at the age of 43, al-Banna was assassinated by government agents following fears about his rising success. For more than 78 years, the Muslim Brotherhood has been active in Islāmic *da`wah* and many other fields. Today, the movement has followers in more than 80 countries around the world.

One word remains: this is a work by a human being, a production of a limited mind and a weak spirit. Whatever in it is beneficial and meaningful is surely the outcome of true guidance from Allāh and whatever looks unsightly is surely my own handiwork. I seek His forgiveness for my mistakes and sinful deeds – surely, there are many of them. I pray to Allāh that He gives you the ability to see the beauty of this work and I conclude by repeating the words recited by the Companions prior to the Battle of the Trench.

Had it not been for You, O Lord!
We would not have been touched by guidance!
Nor would we have prayed!
Nor given charity or gained dominance!

Key to Transliteration

ا	*alif*
ب	*bā*
ت	*tā*
ث	*thā*
ج	*jīm*
ح	*ḥā*
خ	*khā*
د	*dāl*
ذ	*dhāl*
ر	*rā*
ز	*zā*
س	*sīn*
ش	*shīn*
ص	*ṣād*
ض	*ḍāḍ*
ط	*ṭā*
ظ	*ẓā*
ع	*ayn* (indicated with ‘)
غ	*ghayn*
ف	*fā*
ق	*qāf*
ك	*kāf*
ل	*lām*
م	*mīm*
ن	*nūn*
ه	*hā*
و	*wāw*
ي	*yā*
ء	*hamza* (indicated with a’)

Longer vowels are indicated by a stroke over the letter, e.g. ā, ī, ū and Ā, Ī, Ū

Introduction

In the Name of Allāh, the Beneficent, the Merciful

All praise is due to Allāh, the Lord of the Worlds and peace and blessings be upon the leader of devotees, our Prophet Muḥammad and upon his family, his Companions and all those who follow his guidance and strive for the deliverance of his message until the Day of Judgement.

It is the practice of Al-Ikhwān Al-Muslimūn to assemble together one night every week for the purpose of remembering and praising Allāh, whilst also fostering the bonds of brotherhood and togetherness. I wanted to prepare a small treatise to enlighten my colleagues about the merits of *qiyāmul-layl* (night vigil prayers) , the importance of making *du`ā'* (supplication) and *istighfār* (forgiveness) from Allāh – Glorified and Exalted be He. The treatise also includes some well-selected supplications, handed down to us from our righteous predecessors. Such methods used by them remind us of the principles and the etiquettes pertaining to supplication. Given the nature of this small volume, only a few examples of these have been so given.

I turn to Allāh wholeheartedly, yearning for perfect sincerity, guidance and for success to be showered on all of us. Finally, I send peace and blessings to our leader, Muḥammad, his family and all his Companions.

The servant of Allāh,
Ḥasan al-Banna

Chapter One

THE MERITS AND TIMING OF QIYĀMUL-LAYL

My dear brother,

How pleasant it is to seclude yourself – in the dead of night while people are asleep – for the munājah (prayer and supplication) of your Lord. In these blessed hours, the entire universe is immersed in silence, the stars have faded and darkness is everywhere. You rise up with your heart awake to remember your Creator and to acknowledge how insignificant and weak you are and how Great and Mighty He is. Thereupon, you will feel the sweetness of being in His presence. Your heart will find solace in His remembrance and you will attain the joy of receiving His Mercy and Grace. With tears flowing from your eyes, you pray to Him sincerely and seek His forgiveness earnestly. In front of Him, you speak of all your needs, since He is the One Who answers all supplications and fulfils all needs. For when He wills that something should happen, it certainly does. In front of Him you stand in prayer, supplicating for the good of this life and the next, the victory of the cause of da`wah, the realisation of all your wishes and hopes, the safety of your country and the well-being of yourself, your family and your brothers in faith. Victory is sought from Allāh, the Mighty, and the Wise.

Qur'ānic verses

Numerous *Qur'ānic* verses and authentic *aḥādīth* have been reported concerning the merits of this auspicious time. True devotees have always been encouraged to make the utmost use of such times by spending them in various forms of voluntary *`ibādah*. Our righteous predecessors were diligent in not neglecting such great opportunities during which Allāh's bounty is showered in abundance. At such times, they were either occupied with prayer, immersed in *dhikr* or busy with supplication.

Allāh Almighty says in *Sūrah* Āl-`Imrān: "Of the People of the Scripture there is a staunch community who recite the revelations of Allāh in the night season, falling prostrate (before Him). They believe in Allāh and the Last Day, enjoin right conduct, forbid indecency, and vie one with another in good works. They are of the righteous. And whatever good they do, they will not be denied the reward thereof. Allāh is aware of those who ward off (evil)."[1]

In the same *Sūrah*, Allāh says: "For those who keep from evil, with their Lord are gardens underneath which rivers flow, and pure companions, and contentment from Allāh. Allāh is Seer of His bondmen. Those who say: Our Lord! Lo! We believe. So forgive us our sins and guard us from the punishment of the Fire! The steadfast, and the truthful, and the obedient, those who spend (and hoard not), those who pray for pardon in the watches of the night."[2]

In *Sūrah* al-Isrā' we find: "Establish worship at the going down of the sun until the dark of night, and (the recital of) the Qur'ān at dawn. Lo! (The recital of) the Qur'ān at dawn is ever witnessed. And some part of the night awake for it, a largess for you. It may be that your Lord will raise you to a praised station." [3]

And in *Sūrah* al-Furqān: "The (faithful) slaves of the Beneficent are they who walk upon the earth modestly, and when the foolish ones address them answer: Peace; And who spend the night before their Lord, prostrate and standing."[4]

And in *Sūrah* al-Sajdah: "Only those believe in Our revelations who, when they are reminded of them, fall down prostrate and celebrate the praise of their Lord, and they are not scornful, who forsake their beds to cry unto their Lord in fear and hope, and spend of what We have bestowed on them. No soul knows what is kept hidden for them of joy, as a reward for what they used to do." [5]

And in *Sūrah* al-Zumar: "Is he who pays adoration in the watches of the night, prostrate and standing, bewaring of the Hereafter and hoping for the mercy of his Lord, to be accounted equal with a disbeliever? Say (unto them, O Muḥammad): Are those who know equal with those who know not? But only men of understanding will pay heed."[6]

In *Sūrah* Qāf: "Therefore (O Muḥammad) bear with what they say: and hymn the praise of your Lord before the rising and before the setting of the sun. And in the night time hymn His praise: And

1. Āl-`Imrān: 113-115. Translations of the *Qur'ānic* verses with modifications are from Mohammed Marmaduke Pickthall's The Meaning of the Holy Qur'ān.
2. Āl-`Imrān: 15-17
3. al-'Isrā': 78-79
4. al-Furqān: 63-64
5. al-Sajdah: 15-17
6. al-Zumar: 9

after the (prescribed) prostrations."[7]

And: "Lo! Those who keep from evil will dwell amid gardens and water springs. Taking that which their Lord gives them; for lo! Aforetime they were doers of good. They used to sleep but little of the night. And ere the dawning of each day would seek forgiveness."[8]

Allāh enjoins the Prophet ﷺ to be patient and observe the night prayer saying in *Sūrah* al-Ṭūr: "So wait patiently (O Muḥammad) for your Lord's decree, for surely you are in Our sight; and hymn the praise of your Lord when you rise up. And in the night time also hymn His praise, and at the setting of the stars."[9]

The beginning of *Sūrah* al-Muzzammil reads: "O you wrapped up in your raiment! Keep vigil the night long, save a little. A half thereof, or abate a little thereof. Or add (a little) and chant the Qur'ān in measure. For We shall charge you with a word of weight. Lo! The vigil of the night is (a time) when impression is more keen and speech more certain."[10]

In the same *Sūrah*, Allāh Almighty says: "Lo! Your Lord knows how you keep vigil sometimes nearly two thirds of the night, or (sometimes) half or a third thereof, as do a party of those with you. Allāh measures the night and the day. He knows that you count it not, and turns unto you in mercy. Recite, then, of the Qur'ān that which is easy for you."[11]

In *Sūrah* al-Insān, we also read: "Lo! We, even We, have revealed unto you the Qur'ān, a revelation. So submit patiently to your Lord's command, and obey not of them any guilty one or disbeliever. Remember the name of your Lord at morning and evening. And worship Him (a portion) of the night. And glorify Him through the long night."[12]

Prophetic *Aḥadīth*

Abū Hurayrah narrated that the Messenger of Allāh ﷺ said: "When the last third of every night remains, our Lord descends to the nearest heaven and says: 'Is there anyone to invoke Me so that I respond to his invocation? Is there anyone to beseech Me so that I

7. Qāf: 39-40
8. al-Dhāriyāt: 15-18
9. al-Ṭūr: 48-49
10. al-Muzzammil: 1-6
11. al-Muzzammil: 20
12. al-Insān: 23-26

grant him his request? Is there anyone seeking My forgiveness so that I grant him forgiveness.'"[13] Muslim's narration reads: "Allāh waits until the first third of the night has gone by. Thereafter, He descends to the nearest heaven and says: 'I am the King, who is there, invoke Me?'"

`Amr ibn `Anbasah narrated that he heard the Messenger of Allāh ﷺ saying: "The nearest a servant can be to the Lord is in the dead of night. If you can manage to be amongst those who remember Allāh at that hour, do so."[14]

Abū Umāmah said: "It was asked: 'O Messenger of Allāh! Which *du`ā'* is more likely to be answered?' and he ﷺ replied: 'The one that is made in the last portion of the night and after obligatory prayers.'"[15]

Bilāl narrated that the Messenger of Allāh ﷺ said: "Try to practice *qiyāmul-layl* for it has been the practice of your righteous predecessors. It draws you closer to your Lord and protects you against sins. Moreover, it washes off the stains of guilt and protects the body from illness."[16]

Al-Mughīrah ibn Shu`bah said: "The Messenger of Allāh ﷺ used to stand (in the prayer) or pray until both his feet or legs swelled. He was asked why he offered such an unbearable prayer although Allāh has forgiven all his sins. He said: 'Should I not be a grateful servant?'"[17]

`Ā'ishah said: "Never did the Prophet ﷺ miss *qiyāmul-layl*. When overwhelmed by illness or fatigue, he used to pray while sitting."[18]

Ibn Mas`ūd said: "It was mentioned in the presence of the Prophet ﷺ that there is a man who slept for the whole night until the next morning without getting up to pray (i.e. *qiyāmul-layl*). Upon hearing this, the Prophet ﷺ said: 'He is a man in whose ear Satan has urinated.'"[19]

Speaking about Ibn `Umar, Jibrā'īl  said: "He would be such a good man if only he would pray at night!" Informed of this by the Prophet ﷺ, Ibn `Umar kept *qiyāmul-layl* from that day forth. Nafi`, Ibn `Umar's servant said: "Ibn `Umar would pray through the night, then say 'Nafi`, is it the time of *Saḥar*?' When I said 'No' he would

13. al-Bukhārī , Muslim, Mālik, al-Tirmidhī and others.
14. Abū Dāwūd, al-Tirmidhī and al-Ḥakīm and ranked by Tirmidhī as *Ḥasan Ṣaḥīḥ*.
15. al-Tirmidhī who rated it as *Ḥasan Ṣaḥīḥ*.
16. al-Tirmidhī
17. al-Bukhārī, Muslim, Ibn Mājah, al-Tirmidhī and al-Nasā'ī
18. Abū Dāwūd.
19. *al-Saḥīḥayn* (i.e. al-Bukhārī, Muslim) and al-Nasā'ī.

resume his prayers. Then he would ask me again, and when I said: 'Yes' he would sit down and seek the forgiveness of Allāh until the break of dawn.'" It seems that this happened after Ibn`Umar grew old and lost his vision.

Abū Hurayrah narrated that the Prophet ﷺ said: "The best prayer after the prescribed prayer is *qiyāmul-layl*."[20]

According to `Abdullāh ibn `Amr ibn al-`Ās, the Messenger of Allāh ﷺ said: "Whoever recites ten verses of the Qur'ān while performing *qiyāmul-layl*, will never be recorded among the heedless. And whoever finishes the recitation of one hundred verses of the Qur'ān therein, will be recorded among the devout. As for him who recites one thousand verses while performing it, he will be granted heaps of reward."[21]

In the narration of `Abdullāh ibn Hubaysh, the Messenger of Allāh ﷺ was asked "Which of all good deeds is the best?" He ﷺ replied: "Making *qiyāmul-layl* long."

`Ā'ishah said: "The prayer of the Messenger of Allāh ﷺ at night consisted of ten *rak`ah* followed by one odd prostration. Then, he would perform the two *rak`ah* of *Fajr* Prayer making a total of thirteen *rak`ah*."[22]

Abū Hurayrah narrated that the Messenger of Allāh ﷺ said: "When any of you stands up to perform *qiyāmul-layl*, let him commence his prayer by performing two short *rak`ah*."[23]

Traditions of the righteous predecessors

Describing `Alī ibn Abū Ṭālib, Dirar al-Sada'ī said: "He forsook of this world vanity and its allurements and found solace in the solitude of night. I bear witness that I have seen him, when the stars have faded away and the darkness of the night has increased, standing in his sanctuary trembling, weeping and saying: 'O world of vanity and deceit! Try your tricks on someone else! Are you trying to attract me or are you attracted to me? What an impossible task you seek to accomplish; what an outrageous claim. I have divorced you thrice; an irrevocable divorce indeed. Short and sojourn you appear, yet, reckoning is difficult and severe. You are too insignificant to be taking a risk for. Alas! Little are my good deeds,

20. Muslim.
21. Abū Dāwūd
22. al-Bukhārī, Muslim, Abū Dāwūd, Ibn Mājah, al-Tirmidhī and al-Nasā'ī.
23. Muslim and Abū Dāwūd. In Abū Dāwūd's narration he adds: "And let him perform as many *rak`ah* as he wishes afterwards."

long is my journey and frightening is my way.'"

Performing his daily *qiyāmul-layl*, `Umar would be so moved upon reciting a poignant verse of the Qur'ān that he became ill (due to its power). In the silence of the night, 'Abdullāh Ibn Mas`ūd used to get up and recite the Qur'ān and his recitation was such that it sounded like the droning of bees to those who heard it. This was the practice of all the Companions.

Al-Ḥasan was asked: "How is it that those who observe *qiyāmul-layl* possess the most beautiful and radiant countenances?" He replied: "In the darkness of night, they commune with the Merciful and He clothes them in light taken from His divine light."

Al-Rabi` said: "I spent many nights in the house of al-Shāfi`ī and found out that he never slept more than a very short part of the night." Such was the practice of the great Imāms.

While performing his daily *qiyāmul-layl*, Mālik ibn Dinār was reciting the verse that states: "Or do those who commit ill deeds suppose that We shall make them as those who believe and do good works, the same life and death? Bad is their judgement!" (al-Jāthiyah: 21). Touched by the verse, Mālik kept on repeating it until the morning.

Mughīrah ibn Habīb said: "I was at the house of Mālik ibn Dinār one night. When he got up for prayer (i.e. *qiyāmul-layl*), he took hold of his beard and, choking with tears, he began to say: 'O Allāh! Preserve Mālik's grey hair from the Hellfire! My Lord! You know the inhabitants of Paradise and the inhabitants of the Hell-Fire, so which of the two is for Mālik?' He went on saying this until the break of dawn."

After his demise, Imām Junayd was seen in a dream and was asked: "What has Allāh done to you Abul-Qāsim?" He replied: "My complexion has decayed and my knowledge has disappeared, my utterances have been removed and my wit taken away. No deed has shown to be of any benefit except the few *rak`ah* which I used to perform in the depths of the night."

Luqmān instructed his son: "O my son! Do not let the cock become more intelligent than you, for it calls at the time of *Saḥar* while you are asleep."

During these precious times, our righteous predecessors found relief and solace in performing *qiyāmul-layl* that enabled them to forget about whatever pain or fatigue they may have experienced while performing it. Abū Sulaymān al-Daranī said: "The people of the night[24] found more joy during the night than the seekers of lusts and fun (during the day). Had it not been for the sake of *qiyāmul-layl*, I would have never loved living. If Allāh is to give the people of the night as much reward as the pleasure they get when performing *qiyāmul-layl*, they will be receiving an immense reward."

It has been said that nothing in this world is like the pleasures of the Afterlife except the pleasure gained by the people of the night as a result of their secluding themselves for *munājah*.

Muḥammad ibn al-Munkader said: "Nothing of the pleasures of this world (*dunyā*) remains with the exception of three: *qiyāmul-layl*, meeting brothers[25] and performing prayer in congregation."

One of the righteous predecessors said: "For forty years, I have never been saddened by anything other than the break of dawn."[26] Some of our righteous predecessors used to say: "At the time of *Saḥar*, Allāh looks at the hearts of those who are awake and fills it with light. Such hearts will taste the sweetness of this divine light and transmit illumination into the hearts of the heedless."

Describing the pious and the righteous, `Alī ibn Abū Ṭālib said: "In the dead of night, they would be standing on their feet reciting the Qur'ān in a slow measured tone. During their recitation, they lament (due to their sins and wrongdoings) and seek remedy for their maladies.[27] When they recite a verse about Paradise and its pleasures, their souls soar forward (as if) to enter and enjoy its delights. And when they came upon a verse that casts fear in their hearts, they listen tenderly and attentively while imagining that they can hear the terrifying sounds of Hell-fire with their own ears. They bend their backs to bow down, and place their foreheads, their hands and knees on the ground in prostration. They are never satisfied by offering a few righteous deeds and never think of their deeds as being sufficient. Therefore, they always accuse themselves of being negligent and think of their deeds as being unaccepted."

In his *Madkhal*, the Māliki jurist Ibn al-Ḥāj wrote: "There are many benefits pertaining to the performance of *qiyāmul-layl*; it removes sins just as wind removes dead leaves from a tree. Besides, it illuminates one's heart, brightens one's face, wards off laziness, and gives one's body vitality. From the heavens, angels see the person

24. i.e. those who perform *qiyāmul-layl*
25. This is because brothers in faith assist each other to draw nearer to Allāh and enjoin what is good and forbid what is evil.
26. The break of dawn meant the coming of a new day marking an end to *qiyāmul-layl*.
27. For their sins and wrongdoings.

performing *qiyāmul-layl* like a bright star shining on earth. The blessings and the benefits achieved by a person who performs *qiyāmul-layl* are so incredible, magnificent and indescribable."

In one ḥadīth, the Prophet ﷺ is reported to have said: "Truly, throughout the days of the year, there are seasons in which Allāh's blessings and gifts are revealed in abundance. So subject yourselves to the blessings and the gifts of Allāh during such seasons."[28]

My dear brother,

That is how they (our predecessors) were. Therefore, follow their path and adopt their way. They are the ones guided by Allah – so follow them in their guidance. Do not limit your offering of qiyāmul-layl to the night you gather with your brothers. Offer it regularly, for the deeds most loved by Allāh are those that are observed continually, even if they are very few in number. Moreover, know that amongst those things that will assist you in performing qiyāmul-layl continuously and habitually are: sincerity of intention, firm determination, continuous repentance, avoidance of sins and wrongdoing during the day, going to bed early, and, if possible, taking a siesta. Attach yourself to these means of assistance as much as you can and seek Allāh's assistance before all. Draw near to Him and He will bring you closer and closer to Him. Supplicate for His Grace and Bounty and He will surely give you whatever you ask for.

28. An agreed upon ḥadīth narrated by Abū Hurayrah and Abū Sa`īd and reported by al-Ṭabarānī in *Al-Awsaṭ*.

Chapter Two

THE MERITS OF DU`Ā' AND ISTIGHFĀR

There are many *Qur'ānic* verses and Prophetic *aḥādīth* that inform us how virtuous *du`ā'* and *istighfār* are. The following passages are examples.

Qur'ānic verses

Allāh Almighty says: "And when My servants question you concerning Me, then surely I am nigh. I answer the prayer of the supplicant when he cries unto Me. So let them bear My call and let them trust in Me, in order that they may be led aright."[29]

And Allāh says: "And those who, when they do an evil thing or wrong themselves, remember Allāh and implore forgiveness for their sins. Who forgives sins save Allāh only? – And will not knowingly repeat (the wrong) they did. The reward of such will be forgiveness from their Lord, and Gardens underneath which rivers flow, wherein they will abide for ever, a bountiful reward for workers!"[30]

And: "But ask Allāh of His bounty. Lo! Allāh is ever Knower of all things."[31]

And: "Yet whoso does evil or wrongs his own soul, then seeks pardon of Allāh, will find Allāh Forgiving, Merciful."[32]

Allāh the Almighty also commands us to make *du`ā'* in all situations and to supplicate to Him out of fear of His punishment and hope for His reward. He says: "Call upon your Lord humbly and in secret. Lo! He loves not aggressors. Work not confusion on the earth after the fair ordering (thereof), and call on Him in fear and hope. Lo! The mercy of Allāh is nigh unto the good."[33]

Explaining the benefit of seeking forgiveness, Allāh Almighty says: "But Allāh would not punish them while you are with them,

29. al-Baqarah: 186
30. Āl-`Imrān: 135-136
31. al-Nisā': 32
32. al-Nisā': 110
33. al-A`rāf: 55-56

nor will He punish them while you seek forgiveness."[34]

Instructing his people on the importance of seeking forgiveness, Prophet Hūd ﷺ said: "And, O my people! Ask forgiveness of your Lord, then turn unto Him repentant; He will cause the sky to rain abundance on you and will add unto you strength to your strength. Turn not away, guilty!"[35]

Allāh commands us to supplicate to Him saying: "Therefore (O believers) pray unto Allāh, making religion pure for Him (only), however much the disbelievers be averse. The Exalter of Ranks, the Lord of the Throne."[36]

Allāh Almighty also says: "And your Lord has said: Pray unto me and I will hear your prayer. Lo! Those who scorn My service, they will enter Hell, disgraced."[37]

And says: "So know (O Muḥammad) that there is no God save Allāh, and ask forgiveness for your sins and for believing men and believing women. Allāh knows (both) your place of turmoil and your place of rest."[38]

And: "And I have said: Seek pardon of your Lord. Lo! He was ever forgiving. He will let loose the sky for you in plenteous rain, and will help you with wealth and sons, and will assign unto you gardens and will assign unto you rivers."[39]

And finally: "Then hymn the praises of your Lord, and seek forgiveness of Him. Lo! He is ever ready to show mercy."[40]

Prophetic *aḥādīth*

Ibn `Umar narrated that the Messenger of Allāh ﷺ said: "If the gates of *du`ā'* are opened for a person, it means that the gates of mercy have been opened for him.[41] And the most beloved thing which Allāh loves to be asked for is safety. Surely, *du`ā'* helps in alleviating calamities that have already befallen you and protecting you from those calamities that have yet to befall on you. Nothing can stop what is destined (from occurring) except *du`ā'*. So, make

34. al-Anfāl: 33
35. Hūd: 52
36. Ghāfir: 14-15
37. Ghāfir: 60
38. Muḥammad: 19
39. Nūh: 10-12
40. al-Naṣr: 3
41. In *Tuḥfatul-Aḥwadhī* which is an explanation of the *Sunan* of al-Tirmidhī, we read: "That if Allāh guides and gives someone the ability to invoke Him whilst maintaining the etiquettes of *du`ā*, it means that the gates of mercy have been opened for him and that Allāh will either answer his *du`ā* or remove a calamity from him or even increase his reward."

du`ā' frequently."[42]

`Ubādah ibn al-Ṣāmit narrated that the Messenger of Allāh ﷺ said: "If a Muslim supplicates to Allāh for a certain purpose, Allāh will either answer his prayer or remove a calamity that equals the thing he has asked for from Him as long as his *du`ā'* is not meant for committing a sin or severing ties of kinship."[43]

According to al-Nu`mān ibn Bashīr, the Messenger of Allāh ﷺ said: "*Du`ā'* constitutes worship." Then, he recited: "And your Lord has said: Pray unto me and I will hear your prayer."[44]

Anas narrated that the Messenger of Allāh ﷺ said: "Let anyone of you ask Allāh for anything he needs even if he wants to have his torn shoes repaired."[45] In the narration of Thābit al-Banani: "...even if he needs salt or wants to have his torn shoes repaired."

Abū Hurayrah narrated that the Messenger of Allāh ﷺ said: "A person who does not supplicate to Allāh,[46] will find Allāh angry with him."[47]

According to Ibn Mas`ūd, the Messenger of Allāh ﷺ said: "Ask Allāh for His bounty, for Allāh loves to be asked for needs. The best form of *`ibadah* is to patiently wait for relief."[48]

Abū al-Dardā' narrated that the Messenger of Allāh ﷺ said: "If any Muslim supplicates for his brother, (i.e. his brother in Islām), in his absence, an angel will be there saying to him, 'the same be upon you.'"[49]

Abū Bakr al-Ṣiddīq narrated that the Messenger of Allāh ﷺ said: "A man who seeks forgiveness is not a persistent sinner even if he lapses seventy times a day."[50]

Al-Agharr al-Muzanī narrated that the Messenger of Allāh ﷺ said: "My heart becomes clouded and (to remove such clouds) I seek the forgiveness of Allāh one hundred times a day."[51]

In one narration of the same ḥadīth in the *Ṣaḥīḥ* of Muslim, we read: "Return to your Lord in repentance, for by Allāh, I return to my Lord in repentance one hundred times a day."

42. al-Tirmidhī.
43. Ibid.
44. Abū Dāwūd.
45. al-Tirmidhī.
46. i.e. for granting him what he needs.
47. al-Tirmidhī.
48. Ibid.
49. Muslim and Abū Dāwūd who added: "...and Angels will be there saying: '*Amīn*'" (same be upon you).
50. Abū Dāwūd and al-Tirmidhī.
51. Muslim and Abū Dāwūd.

Al-Bukhārī and al-Tirmidhī both reported, on the authority of Abū Hurayrah, that the Messenger of Allāh ﷺ said: "I swear by Allāh's Name, that I seek the forgiveness of Allāh and return to Him in repentance seventy times every day."[52]

Abū Hurayrah also narrated that the Prophet ﷺ said: "When a believer commits a sin, a black spot forms on his heart. If he regrets his sin, mends his ways and seeks forgiveness, the black spot is removed from his heart. But if he goes on sinning and disobeying Allāh, the spot will grow until it covers the whole heart and enshrouds it. Such cover is the 'rust' which Allāh mentions in *Sūrah* al-Muṭaffifīn 'Nay, but that which they have earned is rust upon their hearts.'"[53]

52. al-Bukhārī and al-Tirmidhī ranked as *Ḥasan Ṣaḥīḥ*.
53. This ḥadīth is in al-Tirmidhī who ranked it as *Ḥasan Ṣaḥīḥ*. It is also mentioned by al-Nasā'ī in his *Sunan* and by many others.

Chapter Three

ETIQUETTE AND THE OPTIMAL TIME FOR MAKING DU`Ā'

Numerous *Qur'ānic* verses and Prophetic *aḥādīth* instruct us on how to make our *du`ā'* more likely to be accepted by making it in a way that is loved by Allāh. In our endeavour to gain Allāh's pleasure and have our *du`ā'* accepted by Him, we should be characterised by humility, awe and tranquillity while beseeching the Most High.

ETIQUETTE

Some of the etiquettes that we should observe while making du`ā' are:

1) Raising one's palms

While making *du`ā'*, one is to raise one's palms as if one is receiving something from the heavens. Ibn `Abbās narrated that the Messenger of Allāh ﷺ said: "Do not cover your walls. And whoever looks in a document belonging to his brother (in Islām) without getting his permission, it is like looking into the Hellfire.[54] Make your *du`ā'* while stretching the inner surface of your hands upwards and do not use the outer surface.[55] Once you are done with your *du`ā'*, wipe your faces with it (i.e. your palms)."[56]

54. In *Tuḥfatul-Ahwadhī* this is explained as: "The Prophet forbade us from covering our walls with clothes or garments because this was the practice of haughty people and it involves wasteful spending of money. Scholars' say that a person is not permitted to look at a document that might contain the secret belonging of his brother because this involves unveiling what he wants to hide. Yet, the most correct opinion is that a person is not permitted to look at any personal document belonging to his brother until he receives his permission." This, then, is meant to teach us to seek the permission of others and respect their privacy.
55. While making *du`ā'*, a Muslim is recommended to stretch his palms upwards because the most proper way of seeking bounty is to stretch one's palms humbly to Him so that He fills them with gifts. Yet, if a person is seeking the removal of a calamity or protection against something he fears, he should stretch his hands with their backs upwards, (i.e. facing the heavens).
56. Abū Dāwūd.

2) A presence of heart and conviction that Allāh will accept one's *du`ā'*

Abū Hurayrah narrated that the Messenger of Allāh ﷺ said: "Pray to Allāh with utmost conviction that He will respond to your *du`ā'*. Bear in mind that Allāh does not accept the *du`ā'* of a person whose heart is absent, (i.e. a heedless person)."[57]

3) Praising Allāh

Starting the *du`ā'* by praising Allāh and giving thanks to Him and in addition invoke peace and blessings upon Allāh's Messenger. In the course of his *du`ā'*, a Muslim should periodically also invoke blessings upon the Prophet ﷺ. Faḍālah ibn Abī `Ubayd narrated that the Messenger of Allāh ﷺ heard a person making *du`ā'* during prayer without starting it, (i.e. the *du`ā'*), by invoking blessings upon the Prophet ﷺ. Commenting on this, the Prophet ﷺ said: "Such a man has hastened to his purpose."[58] Then, the Prophet ﷺ called the man and said: "Should any of you make *du`ā'*, let him start by praising Allāh and giving thanks to him. Next to that, he should invoke blessings upon the Prophet and then pray for whatever he wants."[59] According to `Umar, the Messenger of Allāh ﷺ said: "*du`ā'* is kept between the heavens and earth[60] and will not ascend until you invoke blessings on me."[61] In another ḥadīth narrated on the authority of Jābir ibn `Abdullāh, the Prophet ﷺ said: "Do not treat me like a glass of water brought by a rider. Invoke blessings upon me at the beginning of your *du`ā'*, at its middle and at its end."[62]

57. al-Tirmidhī. This ḥadīth demonstrates that a person should be heedful while making *du`ā'* so as to gain Allāh's pleasure. In fact, there is one of three possibilities when a person makes *du`ā'*; his *du`ā'* is answered or Allāh removes a calamity that was to befall him or Allāh holds on to the reward and gives it to him in the Hereafter.

58. This means that the man went ahead to perform his *du`ā'* without making due introduction to it by praising Allāh and invoking blessings upon the Prophet.

59. Reported by the authors of *Sunan* (i.e. Abū Dāwūd, al-Nasā'ī, Ibn Mājah, al-Tirmidhī).

60. i.e. will not gain permission to enter Allāh's presence and that it will be reviewed by Him because it is deficient and incomplete.

61. al-Tirmidhī.

62. This ḥadīth is mentioned in the Arabic version of *Al-Munājah* as a completion for the preceding ḥadīth. However, after due research I have established that these are two separate narrations. The first one is found in the *Sunan* of al-Tirmidhī while this latter in *Majma` al-Zawā'id* by al-Ḥāfiz al-Ḥaythamī. The ḥadīth draws the analogy of a person who leaves invoking blessings upon the Prophet ﷺ with a rider who brings a glass of water and puts it behind him. When he becomes thirsty, he takes a few sips from it. If he is not thirsty, he may use it at the end for his ablution. However, if the water is of no necessity for him at all, he will just get rid of it. Likewise, a person who makes *du`ā'* without invoking blessings upon the Prophet, ﷺ treats him as if he is not that important. Only if he needs him he invokes blessings on him. If not, he will just go ahead with the *du`ā'* without worrying about it. Therefore, the Prophet ﷺ directs us to avoid such undesirable behaviour and receive the benefit of invoking blessings and peace upon him at the beginning, the middle and the end of all our *du`ā'*.

4) Concluding the *du`ā'* with '*Amīn*'

Abū Musbiḥ al-Qara'ī narrated that Abū Zuhayr al-Numayrī said: "One night we went out along with the Prophet ﷺ. We passed by a man who was earnestly invoking Allāh. Thereupon, the Prophet ﷺ stopped to hear what the man was saying and said: 'His *du`ā'* will be answered when he completes it properly'. The Companions asked: 'With what words should he conclude his *du`ā'*, O Messenger of Allāh?' The Prophet ﷺ replied: 'With *Amīn*'. Afterwards, the Prophet ﷺ left. Upon hearing this, the Companions turned to the man saying: 'Say *Amīn* and receive glad tidings!'"[63]

5) A supplicant should be calm and never raise his voice while making *du`ā'*

Abū Mūsa narrated: "We were on a journey when people started raising their voices while pronouncing *Takbīr*.[64] Upon hearing them, the Prophet ﷺ said: "O people! Have mercy on yourselves,[65] for the One you are calling is neither deaf nor absent. Verily, He is All-Hearing and All-Seeing and He is always with you.[66] The One you are calling is nearer to you than the necks of your camels."[67]

6) Choosing short, meaningful and comprehensive expressions (*Jawami` al-Kalīm*)

`Ā'ishah said: "When making *du`ā'*, the Messenger of Allāh ﷺ would choose short and comprehensive expressions of invocation and leave anything other than them."[68]

7) Repeating one's *du`ā'* and *istighfār* three times

Whether making *du`ā'* or seeking Allāh's forgiveness, a person is encouraged to repeat his sentences three times. Ibn Mas`ūd narrated that the Messenger of Allāh ﷺ always loved to repeat his *du`ā'* three times and do the same when seeking Allāh's forgiveness. It has also been narrated that in some situations the Prophet ﷺ used to command them to seek forgiveness 70 times.

63. Abū Dāwūd.
64. i.e. saying *Allāhu-Akbar* (Allāh is the Greatest)
65. The meaning here is not to overburden yourselves by raising your voices.
66. i.e. surrounds you with His knowledge and protection.
67. al-Bukhārī, Muslim, Ibn Mājah, Abū Dāwūd and al-Tirmidhī
68. Abū Dāwūd and al-Ḥākim and ranked authentic by al-Suyūti.

8) A person should be patient in receiving an answer (for his *du`ā'*)

Abū Hurayrah narrated that the Messenger of Allāh ﷺ said: "A person's *du`ā'* is answered as long as he is patient and not trying to accelerate the answer by saying: 'I have already prayed to Allāh, how come that He has not answered my prayer yet?'"[69]

9) *Du`ā'* should always be made for the benefit of the supplicant, his children and his belongings[70]

Jābir narrated that the Messenger of Allāh ﷺ said: "Do not make *du`ā'* against yourselves, your children, your servants or your wealth, for your *du`ā'* may coincide with a time when Allāh the Almighty answers and grants and so it is accepted."[71]

10) Upon making *du`ā'* for someone else, a person should start by making *du`ā'* for himself

Ubayy ibn Ka`b said: "Whenever he wanted to make *du`ā'* for anyone other than himself, the Prophet ﷺ would start by making *du`ā'* for himself."

THE OPTIMAL TIME FOR MAKING DU`Ā'

There are certain times when making du`ā' is more favourable because it is more likely to be accepted then. Some of these times include:

1) Between the *adhān* and *iqāmah*

Anas narrated that the Messenger of Allāh ﷺ said: "*du`ā'* which is made between the *adhān* and *iqāmah* never fails." The Companions asked: "What shall we ask for in such a *du`ā'*, O Messenger of Allāh?" The Prophet ﷺ said: "Pray to Allāh for well-being and safety in this life and in the Afterlife."[72]

69. al-Bukhārī, Muslim, Abū Dāwūd, Ibn Mājah, al-Tirmidhī. Part of having good faith in Allāh and firm belief in Him is to leave things to His Will. It is Allāh who decides when and how something should occur. He knows what is best for us and at what time. Bearing this in mind, a person who supplicates to Allāh for wealth, for instance, should not expect it to happen right away because he does not know what might happen to him if he were given wealth right away. Therefore, he should be patient with the answer and never be in haste, for haste makes waste.

70. This means that one should not make *du`ā'* against oneself or one's children…etc.

71. Abū Dāwūd. The ḥadīth teaches us to make *du`ā'* for good things and never pray for our own harm or the harm of anyone or anything that relates to us. The *du`ā'* might be answered and we regret what we have done. The ḥadīth implicitly teaches us to establish good relations with all those around us as this makes our life better and fuller.

72. Abū Dāwūd and al-Tirmidhī who ranked it as *ḥasan ṣaḥīḥ*.

2) While performing prostration (*sujūd*)

Abū Hurayrah narrated that the Messenger of Allāh ﷺ said: "The nearest a servant can get to his Lord is while in prostration, so make more *du`ā'* while being in such a state."[73]

3) While on a journey and if one is oppressed

Abū Hurayrah also narrated that the Messenger of Allāh ﷺ said: "Three types of *du`ā'* are surely accepted and answered: the *du`ā'* of the oppressed, the *du`ā'* of a traveller, and the *du`ā'* of a father against his child."[74] `Amr ibn al-`Ās narrated that the Messenger of Allāh ﷺ said: "There is no such *du`ā'* that gets Allāh's acceptance faster than the *du`ā'* of a person who prays for another that is not present."[75]

4) When hearing the *adhān*, during war and when it rains

According to Sahl ibn Sa`d, the Messenger of Allāh ﷺ said: "Two things never fail; *du`ā'* (that is) made upon hearing the *adhān* and *du`ā'* which is made during war when the two armies meet each other in combat."[76] In another narration, we read in addition to the above: "…when it rains."

My dear brother in Islām!

During this time of forgiveness and mercy, exert your utmost to make paramount use of time and make as much du`ā' as possible. In the dead of night when everything around you is cloaked in silence, wake up to beseech your Lord for help and His pleasure. In the latter portion of the night and just before the break of dawn, prostrate yourself before Him and ask for His bounty and guidance. Thereupon, you will be showered with mercy, overwhelmed with pleasure and surely be elevated to the ranks of those who gain success in this life and in the Hereafter.

73. Muslim, Abū Dāwūd and al-Nasā'ī.
74. Abū Dāwūd and al-Tirmidhī.
75. Abū Dāwūd and al-Tirmidhī, ranked weak.
76. Imām Mālik's *Muwaṭṭa'* and Abū Dāwūd.

Chapter Four

SELECTED DU`Ā' FROM THE GLORIOUS QUR'ĀN

"Our Lord! Give unto us in the world that which is good and in the Hereafter that which is good, and guard us from the doom of Fire."[77]

"Our Lord! Condemn us not if we forget, or miss the mark! Our Lord! Lay not on us such a burden as You lay on those before us! Our Lord! Impose not on us that which we have not the strength to bear! Pardon us, absolve us and have mercy on us, You are, our Protector, and give us victory over the disbelieving folk."[78]

"Our Lord! Cause not our hearts to stray after You have guided us, and bestow upon us mercy from Your Presence. Lo! You, only You are the Bestower."[79]

"Our Lord! Forgive us for our sins and wasted efforts, make our foothold sure, and give us victory over the disbelieving folk."[80]

"Our Lord! Lo! We have heard a crier calling unto faith: Believe you in your Lord! So we believed. Our Lord! Therefore forgive us our sins, and remit from us our evil deeds, and make us die the death of the righteous. Our Lord! And give us that which You promised to us by Your messengers. Confound us not upon the Day of Resurrection. Lo! You break not the trust."[81]

"Our Lord! We have wronged ourselves. If You forgive us not and have no mercy on us, surely we are of the lost!"[82]

"My Lord! Make me to establish proper worship, and some of my posterity (also); our Lord! And accept the prayer. Our Lord! Forgive me and my parents and believers on the day when the account is cast."[83]

"And say: My Lord! Cause me to come in with a firm incoming and to go out with a firm outgoing. And give me from Your presence a sustaining Power."[84]

77. al-Baqarah: 201
78. al-Baqarah: 286
79. Āl-`Imrān: 8
80. Āl-`Imrān: 147
81. Āl-`Imrān: 193-194
82. al-A`rāf: 23
83. Ibrāhīm: 40-41
84. al-Isrā': 80

"Our Lord! Give us mercy from Your presence and shape for us right conduct in our plight."[85]

"There is no God save You. Glorified be You! I have been a wrong doer."[86]

"My Lord! Forgive and have mercy, for You are best of all Who show mercy." [87]

"Our Lord! Vouchsafe us the comfort of our wives and of our offspring, and make us guides for (all) those who ward off (evil)."[88]

"My Lord! Vouchsafe me wisdom and unite me to the righteous. And give unto me a good report in later generations. And place me among the inheritors of the Garden of Delight."[89]

"Our Lord Forgive us and our brothers who were before us in the faith, and place not in our hearts any rancour toward those who believe. Our Lord! You are Full of Pity, Merciful."[90]

"My Lord! Forgive me and my parents and him who enters my house believing, and believing men and believing women, and increase not the wrong doers in aught save ruin."[91]

85. al-Kahf: 10
86. al-Anbiyā': 87
87. al-Mu'minūn: 118
88. al-Furqān: 74
89. al-Shu`arā': 83-85
90. al-Ḥashr: 10
91. Nūḥ: 28

Chapter Five

ON CELEBRATING PRAISE OF ALLĀH AND INVOKING DIVINE BLESSINGS UPON THE PROPHET

Celebrating praise of Allāh

According to Buraydah, the Prophet ﷺ heard a person saying: "O Allāh! I pray to You while I bear witness that You are Allāh. There is no God but You, the One, The Everlasting Refuge,[92] Who begets not nor has been begotten and there is none like unto You." Upon hearing this, the Prophet ﷺ commented: "By the One in Whose Hands is my soul! This man has used the Greatest Name of Allāh in his prayer. Surely, Allāh answers any supplication and fulfils any need if such a Name is ever used by a supplicant."[93]

Anas ibn Mālik said: "While a man was making *du`ā'*, he said: 'O Allāh! I pray to You (bearing in mind) that all praise and thanks are due to You. There is no God but You, the Most Kind, the Most Bounteous, the Originator of the heavens and the earth, the One full of Majesty and Honour. O Living, O Eternal!' Commenting on this, the Prophet ﷺ asked: 'Do you know with what this man has supplicated?' The Companions said: 'Allāh and His Messenger know best'. The Prophet ﷺ continued: 'By the One in Whose Hands lies my soul, he has supplicated with the Greatest Name of Allāh with which if He was called, He would answer and if He was asked, He would give.'"[94]

Invoking divine blessings upon the Prophet

Abū Mas`ūd al-`Adawī said: "While we were sitting in the assembly of Sa`d ibn `Ubādah, the Prophet ﷺ came to us. Upon

92. The Everlasting Refuge stands for the Arabic word *al-Ṣamad* which is one of the fairest Names of Allāh. In fact, the Arabic word *al-Ṣamad* means more than just an everlasting refuge. Ibn `Abbās said: "*al-Ṣamad* is the One to who people rush to for their needs to be fulfilled and their complaints to be executed and their wishes to be realised. The word also means the Master Who has possessed unsurpassed excellence, the Noble Who has become Himself a source of perfect honour, the Great Whose greatness cannot be rivaled, the Kind Whose kindness overwhelms everything, the All-Knowing Whose knowledge is perfect and unsurpassed and the One Who has no rival or peer." (*Tafsīr, Ibn Kathīr*)

93. Abū Dāwūd and al-Tirmidhī.

94. Reported by the authors of the books of *Sunan*.

seeing him, Bashīr ibn Sa`d asked: 'O Messenger of Allāh! Allāh has ordered us to invoke blessings upon you. How should we bless you?' The Messenger of Allāh ﷺ kept quiet to the extent that we wished we had not asked him. Then he told us to say: 'O Allāh, bless Muḥammad and the family of Muḥammad as You have blessed Ibrāhīm, and shower favours on Muḥammad and the family of Muḥammad as You showered favours on Ibrāhīm. You are indeed Worthy of Praise and Glorious, and then give salutations as you know.'"

`Abdullāh Ibn Mas`ūd said: "When you send blessings to the Messenger of Allāh, do it as perfectly as you can, for you do not know whether or not it may be reviewed by him." People said to him: "Teach us how to do that!" He replied: "Say: 'O Allāh! Shower Your blessings, mercy and favours upon the master of all messengers, leader of all the pious and the seal of prophets, your slave and Messenger Muḥammad who has led people to every good thing and taught them every good deed and given the best example of kindness. O Allāh! Raise him up to the praised position[95] for which all people before and after him long.[96] O Allāh! Bless Muḥammad and his family as you blessed Ibrāhīm and his family. Surely, You are Worthy of Praise and the Owner of Glory. O Allāh! Shower Your favours on Muḥammad and his family as You have showered Your favours on Ibrāhīm and his family. Indeed, You are worthy of all Praise and Owner of Glory.'"[97]

`Alī ibn Abū Ṭālib began one of his sermons saying: "O Allāh, the Spreader of the surfaces (of the earth) and Keeper (intact) of all skies, Creator and Fashioner of hearts the way You wanted them to be, good or evil! Send Your most excellent blessings and eternally

95. i.e. the position of interceding on behalf of his followers on the Day of Judgement.

96. If one feels a great desire for something that belongs to someone else whilst not begrudging that person having this thing, it is called in Arabic *ghabṭah*, which literally means happiness. Such a feeling is Islāmically acceptable because a person who feels that he wants to be as successful as his neighbour, for instance, and at the same time wishes that his neighbour continues being successful has not done anything wrong. However, if one desires to be as successful as one's neighbour but at the same time wishes that one's neighbour fails in everything is surely evil. Such behaviour is called *ḥasad* (envy), which refers to a feeling of discontent and resentment aroused by and in conjunction with a desire for the possessions or qualities of another. This is Islāmically unacceptable and is contrary to having firm belief in Allāh. Envy is not accepted under any circumstances because it contradicts the very feeling of accepting what Allāh has given to each person and consumes a person's heart with hatred and dissatisfaction. All such maladies affect a person's behaviour and spread ill-thinking and malice in society. In Islām, a true believer should have a faithful and pure heart that is swelled with mercy, love and sincerity.

97. *Sunan* of Ibn Mājah, chapter on Blessing the Prophet ﷺ.

increase favours on Your servant and Prophet Muḥammad who is the last of those (Prophets) who preceded him and the opener of what has been closed[98] and the proclaimer of truth with truth."[99]

98. i.e. guidance and revelation. This refers to the fact that the advent of the Prophet ﷺ constituted a new age and his message of Islām represented a fresh link between people and their Creator; a link which had been cut a long time previously. The coming of Islām and the birth of the Prophet ﷺ was, thus, an opening of a closed door and a renewal of this link.

99. From *Nahj Al-Balāghah* (Peaks of Eloquence), a collection of sermons and sayings by `Alī ibn Abū Ṭālib.

Chapter Six

THE PROPHET'S DU`Ā' IN TAHAJJUD PRAYER

`Abdullāh ibn `Abbās narrated that whenever he woke up late at night for the *Tahajjud* Prayer, the Messenger of Allāh ﷺ used to say: "O Allāh! All praise is due to You. You are the Holder of the Heavens and the Earth and whatever is therein. All praise is due to You; You have the possession of the Heavens and the Earth and whatever is therein. All praise is due to You; You are the Light of the Heavens and the Earth and all praise is due to You; You are the King of the Heavens and the Earth and all praise is due to You; You are the Truth and Your Promise is the truth and the meeting with You is true; Your Word is the truth and Paradise and Hell are true and all the prophets are true; and Muḥammad is true, and the Day of Resurrection is true. O Allāh! I surrender (my will) to You. I believe in You and depend on You and repent to You and with Your help I argue (with my opponents). And I take You as a Judge (to judge between us). Forgive me my previous and future sins, and whatever I concealed or revealed, and You are the One who advances (some people) and You retract (some). There is none to be worshipped but You."[100]

100. al- Bukhārī, Muslim, al-Tirmidhī, Abū Dāwūd, al-Nasā'ī and Ibn Mājah.

Chapter Seven

THE MUNĀJAH OF THE RIGHTEOUS

The *Munājah* of `Alī ibn Abū Ṭālib

Abū `Abdullāh Manṣūr ibn Sakbān al-Tustūrī narrated on the authority of Muḥammad ibn al-Ḥasan ibn Ghurāb, Mūsā ibn Isḥāq, Abū` Abdullah Muḥammad ibn Abi Shaybah and Muḥammad ibn Fuḍayl al-Asadi that in his munājah, `Alī ibn Abū Ṭālib used to say:

"My Lord! It is my ignorance that leads me to fall into the abyss of sin, and here I am to complain of my negligence and shed tears at Your door. Wash the stain of sins with the flow of tears; forgive my many evil deeds by increasing the very few good ones!

My Lord! If Your Mercy is only for the good-doer, what can such a poor wrongdoer like I do? If Your help and assistance is only for the pious, to whom do the mischievous go? If, on Judgement Day, only the devout are declared winners, give some hope to the sinners.

My Lord! My words have been severed; I have no argument or excuse. So where should I go with my crime? I confess my sins; imprisoned by misdeeds and indebted by my actions.

My Lord! Bless Muḥammad and the family of Muḥammad and clothe me with Your mercy and cover me with Your pardon.

My Lord! If my good deeds are few and meagre, my hope in You is magnificent. I am sure I will never be an outcast, since Your mercy is great and vast.

My Lord! My hope in You has never been dashed, so crown it with acceptance and never let it be smashed.

My Lord! My crime is great since You are the One Whom I have sinned against.

My Lord! If heedlessness has prevented my preparation for the meeting with You, the knowledge of Your gracious favours has awakened my heart.

My Lord! Had you not guided me to Islām, I would not have been guided. With Your help I am able to celebrate Your praises, and feel the sweetness of Your favours. Severe is Your punishment more than what I know, here I am my Lord crying in front of You.

My Lord! If I am too weak to march with the pious to You, my trust in You places me in the ranks of the righteous.

My Lord! My faith in You clothes me with tranquil attire; how come then that You leave me to the Hellfire?

My Lord! You are the refuge of the distressed and the Everlasting Hope for the sad and oppressed!

My Lord! Hearing of Your mighty reward, the devout strive more, and hearing of Your magnificent forgiveness, the sinners raise their hopes for sure; countless of them are there waiting at Your door. People are everywhere, weeping for Your mercy and praying for Your forgiveness.

My Lord! You told us about the sweetness of Paradise, how great and delightful it is. Coming to know this, our hearts have become attached to it; so do not deprive us from entering it. You are the Source of Generosity and Praiseworthiness, the Owner of Honour, Sovereignty and Majesty.

My Lord! If I am too insignificant to deserve Your mercy, Your mercy is too magnificent and will overwhelm such an insignificant being like me.

My Lord! Here I am standing in front of You, still placing my trust in You, knowing not where to go. Treat me with what suits You, not what suits me and clothe me with the garments of Your mercy.

My Lord! My heart testifies to You being One, on celebrating Your praise my tongue has begun. The Qur'ān is my guide here, and in my heart Your promise resides.

My Lord! Thinking of myself lying in my grave, with none of my relatives around; fearful is my heart and it sinks to the ground. Feeling for my solitude, the angels will cry: 'Stranger is he, in a small pit does he lie. His relatives are gone; left to loneliness around him is none. What helplessness!' My Lord! Being this lost, You are my only host. Be Merciful with me, since my kin have left as You see. Such is my simple plea!

My Lord! You have hidden my misdeeds and covered my back, so scandalise me not on the Day when faces will turn black! I beseech You for favour and ask You for grace, guide me to good deeds, to You direct my face.

My Lord! Help me do things that draw me near to You and avoid those that distract my heart from glorifying You.

My Lord! The best of deeds to me are those You guided me to. No one cares for my heart more than You do! You are the best solace for a stranger, when he feels so torn and lonely. You know the secrets of all hearts, with Your help plight surely departs. I am here alone in the silence of my grave, worn out and destroyed to dust. Have mercy on me, for in You I place my trust. Your bounties have always accompanied me throughout my life; keep them flowing on me also in the Afterlife.

O Allāh! Your bounties are many, countless they are. From showing due gratitude for all of them, my praise and prayers stand afar. All praise is directed to You and all thanks are for You. You are the best to be supplicated, the only One to be beseeched and sought for assistance. You are the Most-Kind, the Most-Bounteous, the Owner of Majesty and Honour, the Living and the Everlasting.

O Allāh! To You belong the Creation and the Command! Blessed be You, the Perfect Creator. You are the Ever-Merciful, the Most-Powerful, and the Most-Generous. Shower Your eternal blessings upon Muḥammad and his devout family! *Amīn*!"[101]

The *Munājah* of Ibn `Ata'illāh of Alexandria

"My Lord! Never will You leave me to my own self, while my trust is placed in You. Never will I be harmed since You are my Protector. Never will I undergo failure, since You honour me with success. Here I am O Lord, here I am! Stricken by poverty, I beseech You. Crippled with sinfulness, I place my hope in Your Forgiveness. My awful qualities vanish when embraced in Your Grace.

My Lord! For a sinner like myself, sins are not strange. For a finite being like me, truths are no more than claims. Your bounties are everywhere, clear for every eye; near to every believing heart, no one can deny. Blind are the eyes that still fail to see You everywhere. Wretched is a person who fails to attain Your Pleasure.

My Lord! Blind is he that forgets You being Witness and All-Seeing. A loser is he who fails to give You his heart in loving obedience.

My Lord! I declare my utter weakness standing in front of You. My state is clear to You. I seek Your help to be elevated to Your

101. Extracted from *Laṭā'if Akhbār Al-Āl* (Glimpses from the Lives of the Family of the Prophet).

presence, beseech Your assistance to be guided to You, shower me with Your Light so that I am blessed by Your Might and place me in sincere servitude in front of You.

My Lord! Enlighten me with Your Ever-Sacred Knowledge and protect me with the secret of Your Most Protected Name. I long for Your assistance so assist me. I place my trust in You, so do not fail me. I beseech You, so do not send me back empty handed. I am here weeping for Your bounty, happy to be Your servant, proud to stand at Your gates, so do not send me away accompanied with failure and disgrace.

My Lord! Your Pleasure is far removed from being the result of a reason on Your part; never can it be the result of a reason on my own part.[102] You are too Divine and Self-Sufficient to be touched by the slightest need. Indeed, our acts of worship are for our own benefit.

My Lord! It is You Who endowed the hearts of Your beloved servants with wisdom until they found their way to You. It is You Who removed all desires and inclinations from the hearts of Your chosen servants until their love became utterly and purely for You. You are their Solace whenever they are cast in the abyss of loneliness and their Beacon in the midst of darkness and their Redeemer from distress.

My Lord! What has the one achieved who loses his way to You and what has the one lost who has found his way to You? Failure is for him who buys worldly allurements in exchange for his bond with You. Loss is his who turns his back on You.

My Lord! How can we turn to anyone else while Your bounties are continuously flowing and overwhelming us? How can we beseech anyone else while Your favours are showered upon us?

My Lord! Your beloved servants have tasted the sweetness of Your pleasure and so they have stood up praying for more. Clothed in the garments of divinely bestowed reverence, Your people move for

102. Here Ibn `Ata'illāh refers to the fact that Allāh showers His pleasure on His servants not because they worship and obey Him but because it is He Who is the Source of generosity and kindness. People may think that Allāh's pleasure is gained when they show obedience to Him. This is of course true. Yet, it does not mean that Allāh's pleasure is in return for their good deeds, simply because it is He Who enabled them to do such good deeds in the first instance. However, Allāh teaches us to strive hard to gain His pleasure and know that in order to gain something, we have to exert ourselves and work hard. This implicitly teaches us to be active and dynamic and put aside laziness and negligence. When it comes to Allāh's pleasure, we are commanded to work hard to gain it. Yet, it is not because of our deeds that Allāh showers His pleasure on us because His pleasure is far removed from being the result of a reason whether on His part or on our part. For it is an original pleasure that comes from the Source of infinite pleasure. It is in no way like our human pleasure, which always related with a reason. For instance, a person says that he is pleased because he has gained wealth or because Allāh is pleased with him. As for Allāh's pleasure, He is the Source of pleasure and there is no place for reasons here.

sure. You remember Your servants long before they think of You. You shower blessings upon us before we ask You to. Your gifts are countless more than what we know.

My Lord! Make Your Mercy my way of finding You and let Your gifts lead me to Your presence.

My Lord! My hope in You is never dashed even if I have disobeyed You and my awe never departs from my heart even if I have obeyed You.

My Lord! The whole world stands as signs of Your Existence and Your Generosity leads me into the gardens of Your obedience.

My Lord! Failure will never befall me since You are my hope. No one can humiliate me, for You are my Protector in this world.

My Lord! Being the Almighty and the Omnipotent, You are hidden from every eye. Yet, Your Majestic Beauty and Greatness are so clear and nigh. You are the Outward and the Ever-Watching!"

The *Munājah* of Aḥmad al-Rifa`ī

"O Allāh! Bless our Prophet Muḥammad, his family and all his Companions. O Allāh! You are the Reliever of distress, the Answerer of the prayer of those in want, and the Merciful of both worlds; this life and the Afterlife. You shower such mercy upon us that we never need mercy from anyone else. There is no god but You, Lord of everything. Glory be to You, there is no god but You. You are the Inheritor of everything. You are the Ever-Living, the Everlasting, the Owner of Majesty and Honour. You are the Most-Merciful, the Most-High, the Great, the Everlasting Refuge, the One and the Only True God. In Your Hand is the good and You have power over all things. I ask You to grant me pure trust in You and complete recourse to You in all situations. I pray to You, Knower of secrets, inner thoughts and feelings. Remover of harm and affliction, to You do the hearts of the afflicted turn in utter submission and to You the hands of the needy are stretched in succession. We ask You Allāh by the might of Your throne, and by the infinite mercy found in Your Book, and by the loftiest of Your Names, and by Your perfect words that cannot be violated by the righteous or the lewd, and by Your Ever-Shining Face, that You bless our master Muḥammad, his family, his Companions and his offspring.

O Allāh! Cherish us with Your secret favours and benevolence so that we are saved in the garments of safety from the afflictions of this material world, its mundane relations, its wicked traps, its failures and misfortunes. Protect us against the wicked tricks of Satan, the ill intentions of our fellow humans and the evil outcome of our sins.

O Allāh! Grant me a heart that never turns with a hope to anyone other than You and a mind that places its infinite trust in You in every encounter. Fill me with knowledge by the merit of my certitude and monotheistic faith. Support me in Your way with things which You provide Your devout servants with. Lead me to the path of Your chosen Prophet Muḥammad. Enable me to show gratitude for Your favours by following his footsteps.

O Allāh! I seek refuge in You from knowledge that does not give me benefit,[103] from deeds that are not accepted, from a heart that is not humble and from prayer that is not answered.

Our Lord! Give us mercy from You and furnish us with rectitude in our affairs. O Allāh! Elevate me by Your Grace to become a true man of Yours.[104] Allow me to taste the sweetness of certitude by the merit of sincere intention and a pure heart. Leave me not to my own self or to any of Your creatures even for the blinking of an eye, O Most-Merciful. No might or power can be gained without (the help of) Allāh, the Most-High, the Great. Peace and blessings shall go to the messengers of Allāh and all praise and thanks are due to Him."[105]

The *Munājah* of Aḥmad ibn Idrīs

"O Allāh! You are the King, the manifest Truth, the Eternal, the Owner of Greatness and Majesty, the Eternally-Subsisting, the Ever-Living, the Sublime Self-Existing, the Supreme Determiner, the Compeller, the Dominator, there is no god but You. You are my Lord and I am Your servant. I have wronged myself by committing an evil deed. Yet, I am here to confess that I have sinned. So, forgive me all my sins, for it is only You Who can forgive sins. I bear witness that You are my Lord and the Lord of everything, the Creator and the Originator of the heavens and earth, the Knower of the Seen and the Unseen, the Great and the Ever-Exalted.

103. i.e. the benefit of being God-fearing and acting according to what one has learnt. In Islām, knowledge and action are closely related. If one gains knowledge, one must apply this knowledge; otherwise such knowledge will be one's enemy on Judgement Day. Allāh will question every person about the gifts He has given to them. When someone is given the gift of knowledge, he has to use it for the benefit of humanity and be a source of goodness.

104. In Arabic, the word *ṣiddīq* has no English equivalent. The nearest meaning is saint, but in Islām, there is no sainthood. Therefore, it is better to use the term true man, since the Arabic word itself is derived from *ṣidq* meaning truthfulness. Therefore, a *ṣiddīq* may be translated as a true man in the sense that he offers many acts of worship with sincerity and is truthful in his devotion; he is, thus, a true man of Allāh.

105. Extracted, with slight modifications, from *Hizbul-Wasīlah* (a collection of prayers and supplication of Aḥmad Al-Rifa`ī)

O Allāh! I beseech You for steadfastness in every affair, determination and resolve in truth, gratitude for Your favours and good devotion[106] to You. I ask You for the good of what You know and seek refuge in You from the evil of what You know. You are the Knower of the Unseen."

The *Munājah* of Shaykh Abul-Ḥasan al-Shadhilī

"O Allāh! You are the Ever-Kind, the Ever-Provider, the Ever-Powerful, the Almighty. To You belongs the control of the heavens and the earth. You outspread Your provision to whom You will and withhold it from whom You will. Outspread to us what enables us to gain Your mercy and shower Your mercy upon us so that we are protected from Your Wrath. Grant us pardon that gives us tranquillity and serenity. Give us happy ends (for our lives) like those which You give to Your chosen people. Make the best of our days and the happiest of them the day we meet You. We beseech You to save us from the flames of base desires and inclination in this life. Embrace us with Your grace to enter into the gardens of Your Mercy. Clothe us with the garments of purity and infallibility that radiate with Your Divine Light. Make our minds our supporters, our souls our companions and our bodies our helpers in our journey to Your Presence that we may celebrate Your praises abundantly and engage in Your remembrance continuously. You always see what is in our hearts.

O Allāh! I beseech You for a tongue that is always engaged in remembering You, a heart that continuously shows gratitude to You and a body that finds its fitness from obeying You. With all this, grant us that which is beyond every human eye, every ear and every heart as said by Your Prophet ﷺ. Grant us provisions from where we perceive not and make us a source of support and richness for Your chosen people. Make us a protection and a veil between them and Your enemies, for You have Power over everything.

O Allāh! I beseech You for perfect faith, a sincere heart, benefiting knowledge, unswerving faith and upright religiousness.

106. Good devotion (*ḥusn `ibādāt*) requires that the ritual itself should be performed according to the way established and demonstrated by the Prophet ﷺ, and that it should be done with sincerity. If pretentiousness occurs in a worshipper's heart, there is no value in his worship. Likewise, if a person contradicts the way set by the Qur'ān or the Prophet's ﷺ example while performing his act of worship, it will not be accepted. In the ḥadīth narrated by `Ā'ishah, the Prophet ﷺ said: "Whoever invents in this affair of ours (i.e. religion) what does not belong to it, it shall be returned back to him" (al-Bukhārī and Muslim).

O Allāh! Grant us safety from every affliction and tribulation and free us from want or need. Habituate our hearts on accepting whatever You decree for us and give us patience and persistence to carry out our duties towards You and restrain ourselves from disobedience and inclination that distances us from You.

O Allāh! Grant us true faith that sets us free from fear of anyone other than You and longing for anyone but You and worshipping anything beside You. Enable us to be thankful for Your favours and wrap us in the cloak of Your safety and well-being. Support our hearts with unswerving faith and complete trust in You. Let our faces shine with the Light of Your Divine Attributes.[107] Smile upon us and grant us glad tidings on the Day of Resurrection amongst Your true men. Shower mercy upon us, our families, our offspring and all those who are around us. Leave us not to our own selves even for the twinkling of an eye or shorter than that. Indeed! You are the best Answerer of Prayers. May peace and blessings be showered in abundance upon our noble Prophet Muḥammad, his family and all his Companions."[108]

The *Munājah* of Imām al-Shāfi`ī

"I seek refuge in You from being degraded to the rank of the ungrateful or being overtaken by heedlessness. O Allāh, for You have the souls of the devout surrendered and for You have the necks of the lovers been advanced. My Lord! Shower me with Your Grace, place me in the garments of Your divinely protected concealment and pardon my negligence by the merit of Your Everlasting Generosity."[109]

107. When a person accustoms himself to Divine attributes and acts accordingly, such attributes make a good person of him. When this occurs, his heart will be pure and enlightened as will be his countenance. For example, when a person remembers that Allāh is the Most Kind and so tries to be kind to everyone and with everything, he will be carrying out, in a sense, one of the Divine attributes. Such kindness, in turn, leaves its impact on his heart and what is in the heart is reflected in the face. Therefore, his countenance will be simple and shining. It is because of this that the Prophet ﷺ instructed us to apply Divine attributes to our lives.

108. Extracted, with slight modifications, from *Ḥibb al-Birr*, a collection of supplications of Shaykh Abul-Ḥasan al-Shadhilī

109. Taken from the *Al-Iḥyā'* of Imām Abū Ḥāmid al-Ghazālī.

Chapter Eight

SELECTED SUPPLICATIONS

Abū Hurayrah narrated that the Messenger of Allāh ﷺ used to supplicate: "O Allāh! Set right for me my religion which is the safeguard of all my affairs.[110] And set right for me this life wherein my living is. Decree the Hereafter, wherein I will be raised up after death, to be set right for me. Make this life a source and store from which I receive more good things.[111] Make death a source of comfort to me and a protection against every evil."[112]

Anas narrated that the most words the Prophet ﷺ used in his supplication were: "Our Lord! Give us in this world what is good and grant us what is good in the world to come and protect us against the torment of the Hellfire."[113]

`Alī ibn Abū Ṭālib narrated that the Prophet ﷺ used to teach some of his Companions to say: "O Allāh! Give us sufficiency and protection in lawful things so that we stay away from that which is prohibited. Shower us with Your Grace and Favours so that we are in no need of anyone."[114]

Abū Hurayrah narrated that the Messenger of Allāh ﷺ said: "Seek refuge in Allāh from the pains of affliction, the depths of misery, the misfortunes of fate and the malice of enemies."[115]

`Abdullāh ibn `Amr ibn al-`Ās narrated that the Messenger of Allāh ﷺ used to say: "O Allāh! I seek refuge in You from a heart that does not feel humility, a supplication that is not answered, a self that

110. A person will find that many a time they are tempted by wrong action and disobedience but due to their truthfulness and deep sense of religiosity they refrain from committing anything that displeases Allāh. Furthermore, when man is in a state of distress and turns to Allāh praying for relief, He grants it to him. In all such situations, religion serves as a safeguard against falling into the abyss of sin or being overtaken by the despair that results from distress.

111. When man is given *barakah* (blessings) in his life, Allāh makes it a source for acquiring further goodness and blessings, which results in more blessings and goodness and so forth. By guiding a person to do righteous deeds, his whole life becomes a source of goodness.

112. Muslim.

113. al-Bukhārī, Muslim and Abū Dāwūd.

114. al-Tirmidhī and al-Nasā'ī.

115. al-Bukhārī, Muslim and al-Nasā'ī.

is not satiated and knowledge that does not yield any benefit. I seek refuge in You from these four (maladies)."[116]

Shaddād ibn Aws narrated that the Messenger of Allāh ﷺ used to say: "O Allāh! I beseech You for steadfastness in all my affairs, determination and resolve in truth. I beseech You for a humble and healthy heart,[117] an upright character, a truthful tongue and accepted deeds. I beseech You for the good things that You know and seek refuge in You from the evil things which You know. I seek Your forgiveness for the sins You know, for You know while I know not. Indeed, You are the Knower of the Unseen."[118]

Mu`ādh ibn Jabal narrated that the Prophet ﷺ used to say: "O Allāh! I beseech You for all lawful things, for doing all good things, for abandoning all evil things and for showing love to the needy. I pray to You to grant me Your love and the love of those who love You and make me love any deed that draws me nearer to Your love. O Allāh! Pardon me and grant me forgiveness and mercy. If You decree a temptation to befall a certain people, then take me to You (in death) untouched by such temptation."[119]

In his *du`ā'*, `Abdullāh ibn Mas`ūd used to say: "O Allāh! Grant me unfailing faith, ever-flowing delight, everlasting satisfaction and allow me to accompany Your Prophet Muḥammad ﷺ in the Gardens of Eternity."[120]

116. al-Tirmidhī and al-Nasā'ī.

117. In Islām a healthy heart is one that is free from clinging to the allurements and delusions of this world. A heart that is free from malice, hatred, envy and all other maladies. A heart may be unhealthy, in terms of physical health, but still healthy spiritually because it is swelled with faith, hope and satisfaction. Many physical problems can be overcome by the merit of having a strong will and determination and a heart that radiates with hope.

118. al-Tirmidhī.

119. al-Tirmidhī and al-Ṭabarānī.

120. al-Nasā'ī.

Conclusion

My dear brother!

It is high time to seek the assistance of your Lord. Voice your needs in front of Him with a full heart and certainty of faith that He will assist you. End your du`ā' with blessings upon the Prophet ﷺ and his family. In order to receive the best reward and excellent recompense, let your last words be the following: "Glorified be my Lord, the Lord of Majesty, above that which they attribute (unto Him), and peace be upon the messengers. And all Praise belongs to Allāh, Lord of the Worlds."

Glossary

Adhān

The call to Prayer. This is the call for people to get ready for prayer and gather at the mosque.

Ākhirah

Literally means 'the other' or 'the end' but is mainly used to refer to 'the Hereafter' or 'the world to come' as opposed to 'this world' or 'the temporary life'. It is even called 'the world to last' as opposed to 'the world to depart'.

Al-Ikhwān Al-Muslimūn

Literally means the Muslim brothers. The name has been adopted by the largest Islāmic movement in modern times founded by Imām Ḥasan al-Banna in Egypt in 1928.

Da`wah

Literally means 'calling' or 'inviting' or 'invitation'. Yet, it is used here to refer to the act of introducing Islām to others. This is not necessarily meant to get others to embrace Islām. On the contrary, it is meant to raise the awareness of non-Muslims about the facts of Islām and its true teachings, so that they can discover aspects of its greatness and so obtain a clear view about it. Some may become fascinated with it and accept it as a course of life, others may prefer to keep their own religion but still show respect to Islām as it shows respect to them.

Dhikr

Literally means 'remembrance'. In Islām, the term *dhikr* covers all feelings, utterances and actions that are meant to celebrate Allāh's praise and express gratitude to Him. It indicates that He is always in a believer's heart. A person is in a state of *dhikr* when he is meticulous in fulfilling his job, when he is good to his Muslim brothers, when he abstains from committing sins all out of fear and love of Allāh. A person can also perform *dhikr* by reciting the Qur'ān, sitting in the mosque to celebrate Allāh's praises, or waiting for the time of the second prayer, helping his brother in Islām, etc.

Dunyā

Literally means 'near' or 'lower'. When we use it without any other modifier, it refers to this 'temporary world' or 'this life' in terms of being near to the person, temporary and sojourn, fake in many of its aspects and not giving real pleasure or happiness.

Du`ā'

Literally means 'calling', 'summoning', 'invoking', and 'supplicating'. Determining which of these meanings is meant depends on the context. Yet, it is used mainly to refer to the earnest and humble request made by a believer calling upon his Creator for assistance at times of need by fulfilling his need, in times of distress by removing the cause of his distress, in times of sadness by relieving him and in times of any difficulty by setting his life right and removing any obstacles from his way. The word is thus used to refer to the action itself and also the set of words used for supplication. Therefore, it covers the process, the action and the formula.

Ḥadīth

The literal meaning of the word involves many things. A conversation between two people is called ḥadīth, a speech given by a person on TV or to the masses is called ḥadīth, a piece of news or a story about a certain event is called ḥadīth. However, in this context and when used without a modifier, it means a saying by the Prophet ﷺ. Sometimes, the word *qudsī* (divine) is added to it to refer to a ḥadīth where the meaning and words are given by Allāh. Yet, when we say 'ḥadīth' without adding anything, it means a saying which is uttered by the Prophet ﷺ in meaning and words. The plural of the word ḥadīth is *aḥādīth*.

`Ibādah

Literally means 'worship' and 'devotion'. However, the Arabic term *`ibādah* is greater than being limited to these two meanings. According to Ibn Taymiyah, *`ibādah* is a title that covers all inner and outer actions and utterances that lead to gaining Allāh's pleasure. Therefore, *Ṣalāh* (prayer), *Zakāh* (alms to the poor), *Ṣawm* (fasting), *Ḥajj* (pilgrimage), truthfulness, fulfilling a trust, keeping relations with kith and kin, honouring parents, keeping one's promises, enjoining what is good, forbidding what is evil, being kind to one's neighbours, the poor and the needy, the wayfarer and even animals are all covered by such a term. In the same way, loving Allāh and His Messenger, being sincere, patient, grateful, hopeful, merciful are all incorporated within the term.

Istighfār

Seeking forgiveness from Allāh by uttering the prescribed *du`ā'* or any words to show that a person is in need of Allāh's forgiveness. It is not only done by the tongue; the heart should also be involved. A person who is seeking forgiveness from Allāh needs to humble his heart to Him, feel deeply remorseful and regret the wrong he has done and the sin he has committed.

Iqāmah

A call to start the actual process of prayer. The time between the first call and this second call is given to Muslims as a space to get ready for prayer by taking ablution, offering some voluntary prayers known as *Sunan* and preparing themselves, physically and spiritually, before standing in front of Allāh in the actual obligatory prayer. While the *adhān* is a call for people to gather and an announcement that prayer time has arrived, the *iqāmah* is a call for people to stand up and line themselves in rows to start the congregational prayer.

Al-Munājah

Literally means 'secret conversation' or 'intimate discourse'. Here, as in many other contexts, it refers to the supplication and prayer done by a believer away from the eyes of others and which is more likely to be sincere and free from any sense of showmanship.

Qiyāmul-layl:

Literally means 'spending the night standing'. It refers to the voluntary prayer that is offered at night. Its time starts from midnight and extends till the time of Dawn Prayer. *Qiyāmul-layl* is normally offered by performing at least two *rak`ah* and then one odd *rak`ah*. One can add as many more *rak`ah* as one wants but one has to end them by offering an odd *rak`ah*.

Rak`ah

Literally means 'one time of bowing down'. The term has been used to refer to the smallest set of actions that formulate a basic unit of prayer. An action like prostration cannot by itself stand as a unit of prayer. Rather, it needs some other actions alongside it to formulate a basic unit. Two of these units make the Dawn Prayer, four of them make the Noon Prayer, four make the Afternoon Prayer, three make the Sunset Prayer and finally four make the Night Prayer. Such are the five prayers required daily of every sane Muslim who has come of age.

Saḥar

This refers to the very late hours of the night that precede the dawn. The time of *Saḥar* is presumably the one to two hours that precede the break of dawn at which time the Dawn Prayer is due. These late hours of the night are the best time for offering voluntary prayer, since a believer has to wake up, refresh himself from slumber, leave his soft bed and stand up for prayer. A believer keeps on praying until the time for the Dawn Prayer is due.

Ṣaḥīḥ

Literally means 'authentic' and 'free from defects'. When used in relation to *aḥādīth* of the Prophet ﷺ, it refers to it being authentic and free from defect.

Tahajjud

This is another name for *qiyāmul-layl*. More specifically, it refers to the voluntary prayer done very late at night, especially at the time of *Saḥar*.